4/21

JOSEPH MIDTHUN　　SAMUEL HITI

BUILDING BLOCKS OF MATHEMATICS

DIVISION

WORLD
BOOK

a Scott Fetzer company
Chicago
www.worldbook.com

World Book, Inc.
180 North LaSalle Street
Suite 900
Chicago, Illinois 60601
USA

For information about other World Book publications,
visit our website at www.worldbook.com
or call 1-800-WORLDBK (967-5325).
For information about sales to schools and libraries,
call 1-800-975-3250 (United States),
or 1-800-837-5365 (Canada).

Library of Congress Cataloging-in-Publication Data

Division.
      pages cm. -- (Building blocks of mathematics)
   Summary: "A graphic nonfiction volume that
introduces critical division concepts"-- Provided by
publisher.
   Includes index.
   ISBN 978-0-7166-1433-3 -- ISBN 978-0-7166-1474-6
(pbk.)
   1. Division--Comic books, strips, etc.--Juvenile
literature. 2. Graphic novels. I. World Book, Inc.
QA115.D575 2013
513.2'14--dc23
                              2012031042

Building Blocks of Mathematics
ISBN: 978-0-7166-1431-9 (set, hc.)

Also available as:
ISBN: 978-0-7166-1474-6 (pbk.)
ISBN: 978-0-7166-7893-9 (trade, hc.)
ISBN: 978-0-7166-1872-0 (e-book, EPUB3)
ISBN: 978-0-7166-2442-4 (e-book, PDF)

Printed in China by Shenzhen Donnelley
Printing Co., Ltd., Guangdong Province
4th printing September 2016

STAFF

Executive Committee
President: Jim O'Rourke
Vice President and Editor in Chief:
   Paul A. Kobasa
Vice President, Finance: Donald D. Keller
Vice President, Marketing: Jean Lin
Director, Human Resources: Bev Ecker

Editorial
Director, Digital & Print Content Development:
   Emily Kline
Editor, Digital & Print Content Development:
   Kendra Muntz
Manager, Indexing Services: David Pofelski
Manager, Contracts & Compliance
   (Rights & Permissions): Loranne K. Shields
Writer and Letterer: Joseph Midthun

Digital
Director, Digital Product Development:
   Erika Meller
Digital Product Manager: Lyndsie Manusos
Digital Product Coordinator: Matthew Werner

Manufacturing/Pre-Press
Manufacturing Manager: Sandra Johnson
Production/Technology Manager:
   Anne Fritzinger
Proofreader: Nathalie Strassheim

Graphics and Design
Senior Art Director: Tom Evans
Coordinator, Design Development and
   Production: Brenda B. Tropinski
Book Design: Samuel Hiti

Acknowledgments:
Created by Samuel Hiti and Joseph Midthun
Art by Samuel Hiti
Text by Joseph Midthun
Special thanks to Anita Wager,
Hala Ghousseini, and Syril McNally

TABLE OF CONTENTS

What Is Division? 4

Three's Company 6

In the Bag 8

Rocks in Boxes 12

Walking Around 16

Camping Out 18

Division in the Wild 22

DIvision and Friends 28

Division Facts 30

Find Out More 31

Note to Educators 32

5

THREE'S COMPANY

Hey Addition!

Hey Multiplication!

What are you up to?

Well, we found some sea shells!

A total of 9!

We are trying to split them up between us!

But we can't figure out how to do it equally!

Why don't I lend you a hand?

Would you?!

We could split the shells between the 3 of us!

That's fine with me as long as we split them equally!

Easy! I would write 9 divided by 3 like this:

9 ÷ 3 = ?

Let's try counting the shells into equal groups of 3 until we run out.

Great idea!

Scoop

1, 2, 3,

4, 5, 6,

7, 8, 9!

plop plop plop

plop plop plop

plop plop plop

Look at this. Now we have 3 groups of 3!

Now, why didn't I think of that?!

When you multiply 3 groups by 3, it looks like this:

3 ✗ 3 = 9

And when you divide 9 into 3 groups, it looks like this:

9 ÷ 3 = 3

I can see you two need a little more practice with dividing!

Let's go!

8

ROCKS IN BOXES

Have you ever seen my rock collection?

No!

I have 15 agates...

Cool!

Psst!

Agates is pronounced "AG-ihts."

Whenever I'm finished looking at my agates, I put them in special boxes to keep them safe.

Each box holds 5 rocks.

So, how many boxes do you need in all?

Hmm.

I can help!

We just need to find out how many groups of 5 are in 15.

We can walk 3 kilometers in 1 hour.

We use kilometers to measure distance.

If we continue on at this pace, how many hours will it take us to walk a distance of 18 kilometers?

We can write the problem as an equation, like this...

$$18 \div 3 = ?$$

Can we use a number line to help?

Sure!

Let's count up by 3 kilometers, or km!

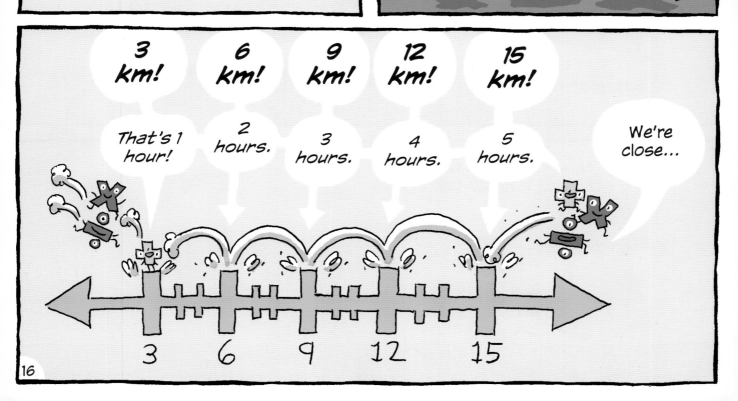

3 km!

That's 1 hour!

6 km!

2 hours.

9 km!

3 hours.

12 km!

4 hours.

15 km!

5 hours.

We're close...

3 6 9 12 15

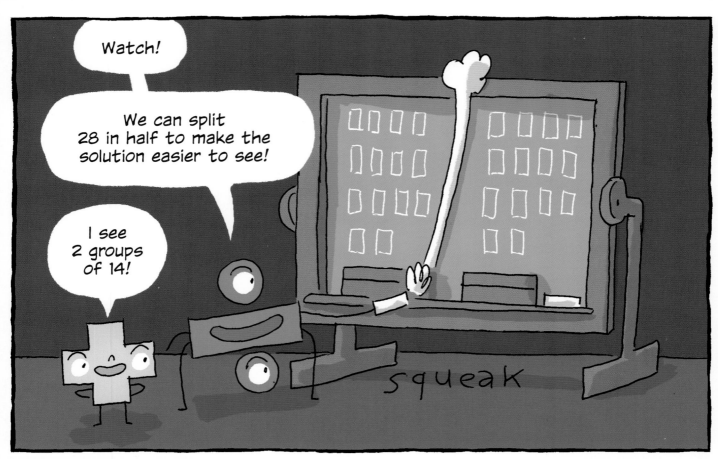

We can use division to find out!

$$35 \div 7 = ?$$

We need to find out how many groups of 7 are in 35. That will tell us how many hours it will take!

Why not count up by 7's on a number line?

Munch!
Munch!
Munch!
Munch!
Munch!

1 hour!

2 hours!

3 hours!

4 hours!

5 hours!

If the grizzly bear catches 7 salmon per hour, it will take 5 hours to catch 35 fish!

7   14   21   28   35

It seems as though this bear has stored up a little extra fat for the winter.

You'd better believe it!

Actually, I've gained 21 kilograms over the past 3 weeks.

Kilograms are a measurement of weight!

If the bear gained the same amount of weight each week, how much did it gain in just 1 week?

Write it like this:

$$21 \div 3 = ?$$

We need to divide 21 into 3 groups. Each group represents 1 week.

Let's use 5-kilogram weights!

PLOP

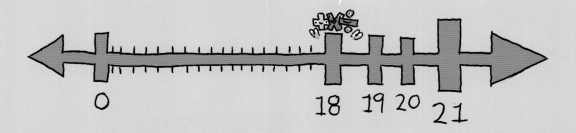

As you can see, there is a lot that you can accomplish with division!

Yeah, even I have to admit, you're pretty complex.

You never know when you might need to use me.

Cough!

Cough!

Cough!

And, if you have trouble when you do, just remember...

...my friends can help.

ZOOP

29

DIVISION FACTS

This table can help you multiply and divide fast!
It can also start you on your way to learning your division fact families.
A fact family shows how groups of numbers are related.

The table shows 10 different fact families for multiplication
and division. Can you think of more fact families?

1 x 1 = 1 1 ÷ 1 = 1	2 x 1 = 2 2 ÷ 1 = 2 2 ÷ 2 = 1	3 x 1 = 3 3 ÷ 1 = 3 3 ÷ 3 = 1	4 x 1 = 4 4 ÷ 1 = 4 4 ÷ 4 = 1	5 x 1 = 5 5 ÷ 1 = 5 5 ÷ 5 = 1
1 x 2 = 2 2 ÷ 2 = 1 2 ÷ 1 = 2	2 x 2 = 4 4 ÷ 2 = 2	3 x 2 = 6 6 ÷ 2 = 3 6 ÷ 3 = 2	4 x 2 = 8 8 ÷ 2 = 4 8 ÷ 4 = 2	5 x 2 = 10 10 ÷ 2 = 5 10 ÷ 5 = 2
1 x 3 = 3 3 ÷ 3 = 1 3 ÷ 1 = 3	2 x 3 = 6 6 ÷ 3 = 2 6 ÷ 2 = 3	3 x 3 = 9 9 ÷ 3 = 3	4 x 3 = 12 12 ÷ 3 = 4 12 ÷ 4 = 3	5 x 3 = 15 15 ÷ 3 = 5 15 ÷ 5 = 3
1 x 4 = 4 4 ÷ 1 = 4 4 ÷ 4 = 1	2 x 4 = 8 8 ÷ 4 = 2 8 ÷ 2 = 4	3 x 4 = 12 12 ÷ 4 = 3 12 ÷ 3 = 4	4 x 4 = 16 16 ÷ 4 = 4	5 x 4 = 20 20 ÷ 4 = 5 20 ÷ 5 = 4
1 x 5 = 5 5 ÷ 1 = 5 5 ÷ 5 = 1	2 x 5 = 10 10 ÷ 5 = 2 10 ÷ 2 = 5	3 x 5 = 15 15 ÷ 5 = 3 15 ÷ 3 = 5	4 x 5 = 20 20 ÷ 5 = 4 20 ÷ 4 = 5	5 x 5 = 25 25 ÷ 5 = 5

FIND OUT MORE

BOOKS

Cheetah Math: Learning About Division from Baby Cheetahs
by Ann Whitehead Nagda
(Henry Holt, 2007)

Divide and Ride
by Stuart J. Murphy
(HarperCollins Publishers, 1997)

Divide It Up
by Tonya Leslie and Ari Ginsburg
(Children's Press, 2005)

Dividing Treasures
by Loren I. Charles
(Capstone Press, 2011)

Division Made Easy
by Rebecca Wingard-Nelson
and Tom LaBaff
(Enslow Elementary, 2005)

The Great Divide
by Danielle Carroll
(Yellow Umbrella Books, 2006)

If You Were a Divided-By Sign
by Trisha Speed Shaskan
and Sarah Dillard
(Picture Window Books, 2009)

Mathemagic! Number Tricks
by Lynda Colgan and others
(Kids Can Press, 2011)

WEBSITES

ABCYa! Division Drag Race
http://www.abcya.com/
division_drag_race.htm
The faster you can divide, the faster you
can drive in this practice game.

Division Games
http://www.divisiongames.net/
Arcade games at this site let you battle
invaders from space with your sharp
division skills!

Fun 4 the Brain: Division
http://www.fun4thebrain.com/division.html
Pick up essential division skills with the
games and printable worksheets at this
educational website.

Kids' Numbers: Division
http://www.kidsnumbers.com/division.php
Build strong division skills with lessons and
games that go week by week.

My Math Games: Division
http://www.learninggamesforkids.com/
math_division_games.html
Practice your division facts with flash
cards and games.

Play Kids' Games: Math Games
http://www.playkidsgames.com/
mathGames.htm
Test all of your math skills with this
site's wide variety of games.

NOTE TO EDUCATORS

This volume supports a conceptual understanding of division through a series of story problems. As Division and the other operations characters work to solve each story problem, they present different strategies, including variations of direct modeling, counting, and invented strategies. Below is an index of strategies that appear in this volume. For more information about how to use these strategies in the classroom, see the list of Educator Resources at the bottom of this page.

Index of Strategies

Direct modeling..6-7; 10-11; 12-13
Repeated halving......................................20-21
Repeated subtraction...........................14-15
Skip counting.............................10-11; 16-17; 23
Trial and error....................................8-9; 10-11; 24-25
Using multiplication facts......................26-27

Educator Resources

Children's Mathematics: Cognitively Guided Instruction
   by Thomas Carpenter, Elizabeth Fennema, Megan L. Franke, Linda Levi, and Susan B. Empson (Heinemann, 1999)

Elementary and Middle School Mathematics: Teaching Developmentally
   by John A. Van de Walle, Karen S. Karp, and Jennifer M. Bay-Williams (Harcourt, 2013)

Knowing and Teaching Elementary Mathematics: Teachers' Understanding of Fundamental Mathematics in China and the United States
   by Liping Ma (Routledge, 2010)

**Young Mathematicians at Work:
Constructing Multiplication and Division**
   by Catherine Twomey Fosnot and Maarten Dolk (Heinemann, 2001)